D0604441

The OVIRAPTOR ADVENTURE

Mark Norell and the Egg Thief

by Meish Goldish

Consultant: Dr. Luis M. Chiappe, Director
The Dinosaur Institute
Natural History Museum of Los Angeles County

BEARPORT
PUBLISHING

New York, New York

Credits

Cover, Charlie McGrady Studio; Title Page, Louie Psihoyos / Science Faction; 4, © Louie Psihoyos / Science Faction; 5, © Mick Ellison; 6, © Neg. #258467, American Museum of Natural History; 7, © Neg. #219165, American Museum of Natural History; 8, © Neg. #410767, American Museum of Natural History; 9, © Neg. #110266, American Museum of Natural History; 10, © Neg. #410944, American Museum of Natural History; 11T, © Mick Elliison; 11B, © Louie Psihoyos / Science Faction; 12, © Mick Ellison; 13T, © Neg. #410737s / American Museum of Natural History; 13B, © Charlie McGrady Studio; 14, © Neg. #410761 / American Museum of Natural History; 15, © Neg. #410765s / American Museum of Natural History; 16, © Neg. #313658 / American Museum of Natural History; 17, © Christian Darkin / Photo Researchers, Inc.; 18, © Mick Ellison; 19, © Mick Ellison; 20–21, © Louie Psihoyos / Science Faction; 21, © Mick Ellison; 22T, © American Museum of Natural History / Science Faction; 22B, © Mick Ellison; 23, © Mick Ellison; 24, Kathrin Ayer; 25, © Louie Psihoyos / Science Faction; 26, © Michel & Christine Denis-Huot / Photo Researchers, Inc.; 27, © Reuters / Corbis; 28–29, Rodica Prato; 28, © Joe Tucciarone; 29T, © Luis V. Rey; 29B, © Natural History Museum Picture Library, London.

Publisher: Kenn Goin; Editorial Director: Adam Siegel; Editorial Development: Natalie Lunis; Creative Director: Spencer Brinker; Photo Researcher: Beaura Kathy Ringrose; Design: Dawn Beard Creative

Special thanks to Emily Lanzara at the American Museum of Natural History

Library of Congress Cataloging-in-Publication Data
Goldish, Meish.
    The oviraptor adventure : Mark Norell and the egg thief / by Meish Goldish.
       p. cm. — (Fossil hunters)
    Includes bibliographical references and index.
    ISBN-13: 978-1-59716-258-6 (library binding)
    ISBN-10: 1-59716-258-2 (library binding)
    ISBN-13: 978-1-59716-286-9 (pbk.)
    ISBN-10: 1-59716-286-8 (pbk.)
    1. Oviraptor—Eggs—Mongolia—Juvenile literature. 2. Oviraptor—Nests—Mongolia—Juvenile literature.
I. Norell, Mark. II. Title. III. Series.

QE862.S3G66 2007
567.912—dc22

2006008000

For more information, write to Bearport Publishing Company, Inc., 101 Fifth Avenue, Suite 6R, New York, New York 10003. Printed in the United States of America.

10 9 8 7 6 5 4 3 2 1

Table of Contents

A Shocking Discovery

Deep in the Gobi (GOH-bee) Desert, Mark Norell was hunting for **fossils**. As he searched the dry, rocky ground, he spotted a nest of dinosaur eggs. One egg caught his eye. The top was worn away. Inside the shell was a tiny dinosaur skeleton.

Mark Norell in the Gobi Desert using a pick to uncover dinosaur eggs

Mark could hardly believe his eyes. The dinosaur inside was not the kind he expected to see. This egg would change everything. A great mystery would finally be solved.

Mark and his team were searching for dinosaurs in an area of the Gobi Desert called Ukhaa Tolgod, which means "brown hills."

Dinosaurs lived in the Gobi Desert tens of millions of years ago. Sand and rock have preserved their eggs to this day.

Back to the Beginning

The dinosaur egg mystery began 70 years earlier. In 1922, a team of **paleontologists** traveled to Mongolia. They were led by Roy Chapman Andrews, who worked at the American Museum of Natural History in New York City.

Andrews loved to explore new places. "I was born to be an explorer," he once said.

Roy Chapman Andrews

Andrews began his career at the American Museum of Natural History as a janitor. He said it was an honor just to clean the floors there.

Andrews had good reason for going to Mongolia. He wished to explore the Gobi Desert. He wanted to search for **ancient** bones of people and animals.

Some scientists believed Mongolia was the home of the first people on Earth. Andrews was eager to find out if that was true.

Before Andrews searched for dinosaur bones, he had recovered and studied whale skeletons. He sailed on Japanese whaling boats to learn more about the animals.

Cars and Camels

Andrews's **expedition** took a lot of planning. Cars and trucks carried the team across the Gobi. The desert had no gas stations, so camels carried extra gas. The animals walked ahead and left the gas at spots where the **vehicles** could fill up later. The camels also carried food, clothing, and equipment.

Andrews's team of camels carried equipment that weighed more than 36,000 pounds (16,329 kg).

Andrews traveled with about 40 people. Some were American and British scientists. Others were Mongolians who knew the desert well.

The Mongols were fascinated by Andrews and his expedition. They had never seen cars before. They called Andrews a "dragon hunter" because he searched for the bones of strange, ancient animals.

Camels carried spare tires for cars and trucks.

Dangers in the Desert

Exploring the desert wasn't easy. During the day, the temperature rose to well over 100°F (38°C). At night, it dropped down to freezing.

Sand was also a serious problem. Powerful **sandstorms** struck without warning. The flying sand damaged car windshields. It also got into people's hair and clothing and tore at their skin.

Cars in the desert often got stuck in the sand and had to be pushed out.

The desert had other dangers as well. **Poisonous** snakes crawled into the tents after dark. **Bandits** would sometimes try to rob the scientists. Andrews always carried two guns for protection.

The Gobi Desert is famous for its powerful sandstorms. They can often last as long as ten days.

Fossil hunters protect their eyes during a sandstorm in the Gobi.

11

A Dinosaur Graveyard

Andrews came to a hilly part of the Gobi. The hot desert sun shone on the cliffs. It made the rock glow like fire. Andrews called the area the Flaming Cliffs.

Andrews and his team searched for the bones of ancient people. They never found any, but they did uncover something else—dinosaur bones.

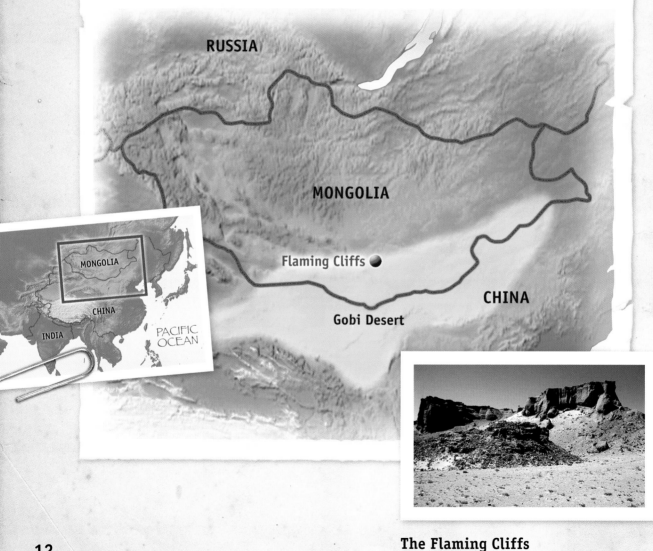

The Flaming Cliffs

The team found fossils of a new kind of plant-eating dinosaur. Its skull had a small horn. The dinosaur was named *Protoceratops* (*proh*-toh-SAIR-uh-tops), which means "first horned face."

Andrews and his team discovered the bones of many more *Protoceratops*. Hundreds of these dinosaurs had lived and died in the area. The Flaming Cliffs was a dinosaur graveyard!

Many *Protoceratops* skulls, such as this one, were uncovered at the Flaming Cliffs.

Protoceratops's official name is *Protoceratops andrewsi*. It was named partly for Andrews.

This model shows what an adult *Protoceratops* might have looked like.

A Fantastic Find

Andrews's team was excited to find *Protoceratops*. Their next discovery was even more exciting, though. In 1923, the team uncovered fossil eggs. At first, no one knew what kind they were. Were they bird eggs? They were too large to be lizard eggs. The scientists soon realized they were dinosaur eggs!

Andrews (left) and a nest of dinosaur eggs at the Flaming Cliffs

The eggs were extremely important. They were some of the first dinosaur eggs ever found in the world. Until then, scientists weren't even sure if dinosaurs laid eggs. The discovery at the Flaming Cliffs proved that they did.

The team continued their search. They uncovered many more dinosaur eggs in the area.

The dinosaur eggs looked like baked potatoes with wrinkled skins.

Some of the dinosaur eggs found by Andrews's team are now on display at the American Museum of Natural History. Visitors can even touch one of them.

A Thief Is Caught

One day, Andrews's team uncovered a nest of dinosaur eggs. On top of the eggs were the bones of a dinosaur. The bones didn't belong to *Protoceratops*, however.

Andrews and his team faced a mystery: Who had laid these eggs? When the fossils were shipped back to New York, paleontologists studied them. They knew that many *Protoceratops* bones had been found near the eggs. So they decided that the eggs must belong to *Protoceratops*.

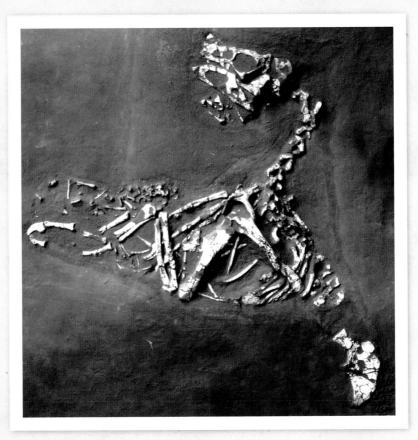

The bones of this dinosaur were found by Andrews's team on top of a nest of eggs.

Another question remained: Whose bones lay on top of the nest? The animal's sharp claws showed that it was a meat-eating dinosaur. It seemed that the creature had been stealing and eating the *Protoceratops* eggs. So the dinosaur was named *Oviraptor* (*oh*-vih-RAP-tur), which means "egg thief."

An illustration of two *Oviraptors* about to eat some *Protoceratops* eggs

Oviraptor and the nest of eggs were probably buried by the collapse of a giant **sand dune**.

A Second Search

For 70 years, paleontologists thought that *Oviraptor* was an egg thief. Yet ideas in science can change. New discoveries can bring new ways of thinking.

In 1993, a new expedition set out for Mongolia. One of the leaders was Mark Norell. He wanted to see what his team would find in the Gobi Desert.

Mark Norell has explored many parts of the world in search of fossils, including South America's Andes Mountains, West Africa, and northern China.

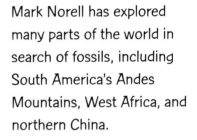

Mark Norell in a fossil quarry in China

Mark was like Andrews in many ways. He worked at the American Museum of Natural History. He loved to explore and to discover new things.

Mark planned his trip carefully. "The best discoveries are those that come out of long planning and a lot of work," he said.

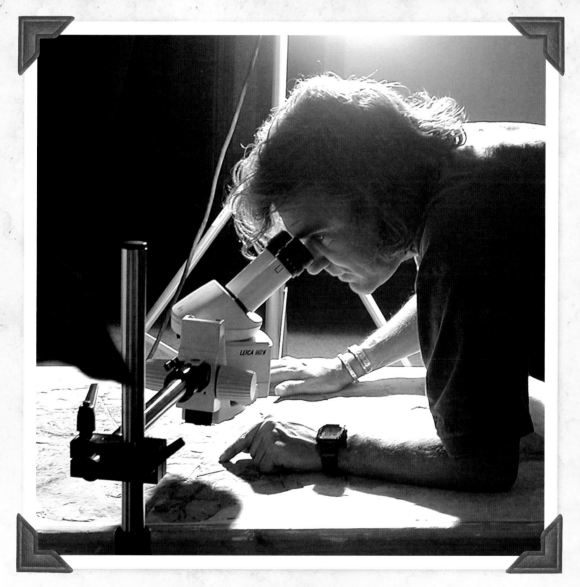

When he is not on an expedition, Mark studies fossils that have already been found.

The Same But Different

Mark and his team traveled toward the middle of the Gobi Desert. In some ways, the trip was just like Andrews's expedition. The team passed through the same areas and faced the same desert heat. They battled rough sandstorms. Luckily, they didn't run into any bandits.

Mark and his team traveled in sturdy vehicles.

In other ways, though, Mark's expedition was different from Andrews's. Mark didn't have a **caravan** of camels. Some team members rode in an army truck, while others traveled in well-built cars. A gas tanker followed to supply **fuel** when vehicles ran low.

Mark worked with modern equipment. His team used computers and walkie-talkies.

Mark's team digging out fossils in the Gobi

In 1923, Andrews had shot **antelope** for dinner. In 1993, Mark and his team ate freeze-dried meat.

Tiny Bones and Big Bones

In the desert, Mark's team found lots of *Protoceratops* bones. They also uncovered dinosaur eggs. They looked like the ones Andrews's team had found in 1923.

In one nest, Mark saw an egg that was open on top. He looked closely. Inside were the tiny bones of an unborn baby dinosaur. He couldn't tell exactly what kind, but he knew it wasn't a *Protoceratops*.

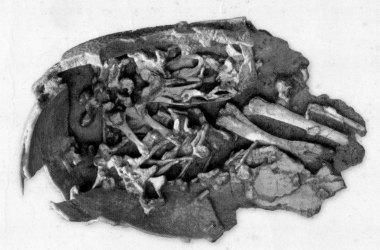

Mark found the bones of this unborn dinosaur inside its shell.

Mark could tell the unborn baby dinosaur was not a *Protoceratops* because it had only three toes on each foot. *Protoceratops* had five toes.

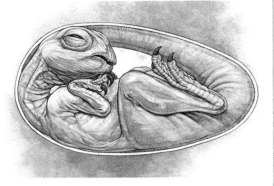

This drawing shows what the unborn dinosaur might have looked like before it died and left only its bones.

Mark's team found the bones of an adult dinosaur on top of another nest of eggs. The dinosaur looked like an **oviraptorid**—a meat-eating dinosaur that belonged to the same family as *Oviraptor*. Was this another "thief" trying to steal eggs?

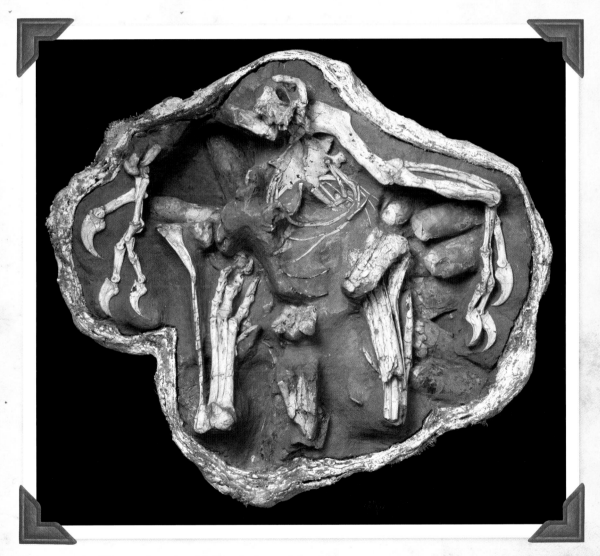

The oviraptorid Mark found had its arms wrapped around a nest of eggs.

A Mystery Is Solved

Back in New York, Mark and the other paleontologists identified the dinosaur inside the egg. It was an oviraptorid. They also realized that the adult oviraptorid Mark found on top of a nest wasn't stealing eggs. It was sitting on its own eggs.

From *Oviraptor* to Fossil

1 **While sitting on its nest of eggs, *Oviraptor* died and was buried by sand.**

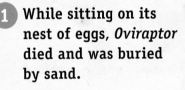

2 ***Oviraptor*'s soft parts, such as its flesh and eyes, rotted away. Its bones, teeth, and eggs survived as fossils for millions of years.**

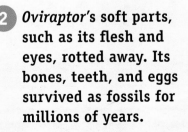

Finally everything made sense to Mark. A huge mistake had been made 70 years earlier. The *Oviraptor* that Andrews and his team found hadn't been stealing *Protoceratops* eggs. It had been protecting its own eggs.

Oviraptor had been given an unfair name. It wasn't an egg thief at all. It was simply a good parent.

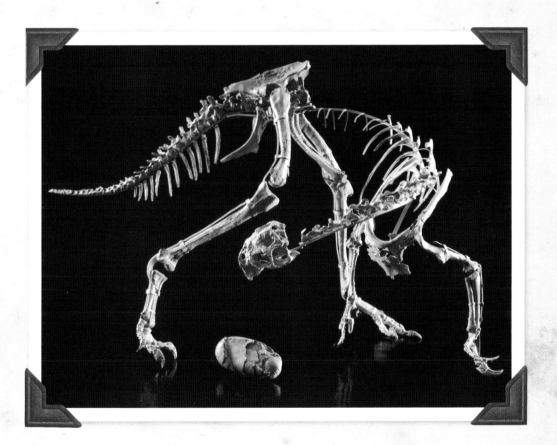

3 An *Oviraptor* skeleton and egg is displayed at a museum.

Mark and his team named the oviraptorid they found *Citipati*. They also gave it a nickname— "Big Mama."

Dinosaurs and Birds

Mark's discovery suggested that *Oviraptor* was a good parent. It also suggested that the dinosaur behaved like a bird. *Oviraptor* sat on its nest, **brooding** and protecting its eggs. Mark's new finding added to an old debate: Are today's birds the **descendants** of dinosaurs?

Some dinosaurs, such as *Oviraptor*, may have sat on top of a nest of eggs the way birds do today.

Many scientists think birds may have come from dinosaurs. Their skulls, claws, legs, and tails are similar. So are their eggshells. Some dinosaurs even had feathers. Mark Norell hopes to find more evidence that connects dinosaurs and birds. By exploring, he hopes to dig up the facts.

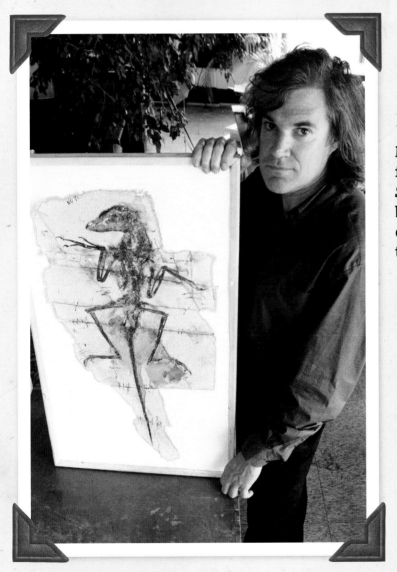

Mark is holding up the fossil of a dinosaur, *Sinornithosaurus*, whose body was probably covered with feathers to keep it warm.

Bird skeletons and dinosaur skeletons have more than 125 features in common.

A Trip Back in Time: Who Lived with *Oviraptor*?

Dinosaurs lived on Earth for around 150 million years. Scientists divide the time in which the dinosaurs lived into three periods—the Triassic period (250 to 205 million years ago), the Jurassic period (205 to 145 million years ago), and the Cretaceous period (145 to 65 million years ago).

Oviraptor and *Protoceratops* lived near the end of the Cretaceous period. Here are three dinosaurs that lived at the same time and in the same places as they did.

Velociraptor

This meat-eater was made famous in the movie *Jurassic Park*. It was similar to *Oviraptor* in many ways, although it was somewhat smaller.

FACTS

Velociraptor
(vuh-*loss*-uh-RAP-tur)

- name means "swift thief"
- had long, flexible arms and powerful feet with sharp, deadly claws
- used its long, straight tail for balance when running and kicking
- **size:** 6 feet (1.8 m) long

Saurornithoides

This meat-eater probably also had a lot in common with *Oviraptor*. Its fossils are much rarer, though. Only its skull, a few arm and hip bones, and teeth have been discovered so far.

FACTS

Saurornithoides
(sor-*or*-nih-THOI-deez)

- name means "lizard-bird form"
- had a long, narrow skull resembling that of a bird
- also had long, powerful arms and three-fingered hands to grab prey
- probably hunted small mammals and reptiles, with the help of its excellent sight and hearing
- **size:** 7 feet (2 m) long

Pinacosaurus

This plant-eater belonged to a group of dinosaurs called ankylosaurs (AN-kee-luh-*sorz*). The upper part of an ankylosaur's body was covered with an armor of bony plates.

FACTS

Pinacosaurus
(pin-*ah*-koh-SOR-uhss)

- name means "plank lizard"
- like other ankylosaurs, it had a club-shaped tail
- moved its tail from side to side for protection in an attack
- **size:** 18 feet (5.4 m) long

Glossary

ancient (AYN-shunt)
very old

antelope (AN-tuh-lope)
animals related to goats and
oxen, with long legs and
hollow horns

bandits (BAN-dits)
robbers

brooding (BROOD-ing)
sitting on eggs before they
hatch to keep them warm

caravan (KA-ruh-*van*)
a group of vehicles or animals
traveling together

descendants (di-SEND-uhnts)
people or animals that come
from a family that lived earlier
in time

expedition (*ek*-spuh-DISH-uhn)
a long trip taken for a specific
reason, such as exploring

fossils (FOSS-uhlz)
what is left of plants or
animals that lived long ago

fuel (FYOO-uhl)
something that is used as a
source of energy or heat, such
as gasoline

oviraptorid (*oh*-vih-RAP-tur-id)
one of a group of meat-eating
dinosaurs that had feathers,
wing-like arms, and usually a
toothless beak; it lived mainly
in the Cretaceous period, and
most of its fossils have been
found in Asia

paleontologists
(pale-ee-uhn-TOL-uh-jists)
scientists who learn about
ancient life by studying fossils

poisonous (POI-zuhn-uhss)
having a substance that can
harm or kill

sand dune (SAND DOON)
a hill of sand made by the wind

sandstorms (SAND-stormz)
windstorms that make sand fly
through the air

vehicles (VEE-uh-kuhlz)
machines, such as cars and
trucks, that carry people
or goods from one place to
another

Bibliography

Bausum, Ann. *Dragon Bones and Dinosaur Eggs: A Photobiography of Explorer Roy Chapman Andrews.* Washington, D.C.: The National Geographic Society (2000).

Gallenkamp, Charles. *Dragon Hunter: Roy Chapman Andrews and the Central Asiatic Expeditions.* New York: Penguin Books (2001).

Holmes, Thom, and Laurie Holmes. *Great Dinosaur Expeditions and Discoveries: Adventures with the Fossil Hunters.* Berkeley Heights, NJ: Enslow Publishers (2003).

Lessem, Don. *Raptors! The Nastiest Dinosaurs.* Boston: Little, Brown and Company (1998).

Norell, Mark, Lowell Dingus, and Eugene Gaffney. *Discovering Dinosaurs: Evolution, Extinction, and the Lessons of Prehistory.* Los Angeles: University of California Press (2000).

Read More

Floca, Brian. *Dinosaurs at the Ends of the Earth: The Story of the Central Asiatic Expeditions.* New York: DK Publishing (2000).

Marrin, Albert. *Secrets from the Rocks: Dinosaur Hunting with Roy Chapman Andrews.* New York: Dutton Children's Books (2002).

Norell, Mark A., and Lowell Dingus. *A Nest of Dinosaurs: The Story of Oviraptor.* New York: Doubleday (1999).

Rey, Luis V. *Extreme Dinosaurs.* San Francisco: Chronicle Books (2001).

Tanaka, Shelley. *Graveyards of the Dinosaurs.* New York: Hyperion/ Madison Press Book (1998).

Learn More Online

Visit these Web sites to learn more about Mark Norell and *Oviraptor*:

http://teacher.scholastic.com/researchtools/articlearchives/dinos/dinoegg.htm

http://yahooligans.yahoo.com/content/science/dinosaurs/dino_card/32.html

www.enchantedlearning.com/subjects/dinosaurs/dinos/Oviraptor.shtml

Index

About the Author

Meish Goldish has written more than 100 books for
children. His book *Fossil Tales* won the Learning
Magazine Teachers' Choice Award.